Twenty Names in THEATRE

Robert James

Illustrated by Gillian Andrae

Wayland

Twenty Names

Twenty Names in Art
Twenty Names in Aviation
Twenty Campaigners for Change
Twenty Names in Classical Music
Twenty Names in Crime
Twenty Explorers
Twenty Names in Films
Twenty Inventors
Twenty Names in Medicine
Twenty Names in Modern Literature
Twenty Novelists
Twenty Names in Pop Music
Twenty Names in Space Exploration
Twenty Names in Sport
Twenty Names in Theatre
Twenty Tyrants

Editor: Alison Cooper

First published in 1989 by
Wayland (Publishers) Limited
61 Western Road, Hove
East Sussex BN3 1JD, England

British Library Cataloguing in Publication Data
James, Robert
Twenty names in theatre.
1.Theatre, to 1988. Biographies. Collections
2.Drama, to 1988.Biographies.Collections
I.Title II.Andrae, Gillian III.Series
792.'092'2

ISBN 1-85210-602-6

Typeset by Lizzie George, Wayland
Printed in Italy by G. Canale C.S.p.A.,Turin
Bound in Britain at The Bath Press, Avon

Contents

The art of theatre

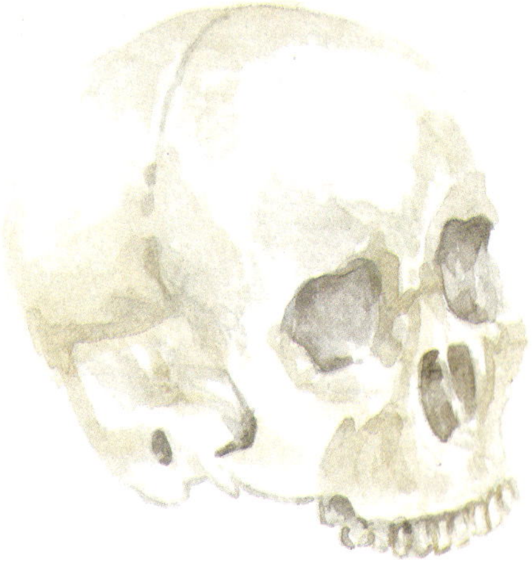

The theatre is the most complex of all the arts. It depends on having a play, a director, a group of actors, a scenic designer, and often a composer of incidental music. However, when all these elements come together in one place at a certain time, great theatrical occasions may occur.

The playwright is the most important and creative figure in the theatre, supplying the ideas behind a piece of work and setting the theme of a play. Without a play, a show cannot be performed. But because the play is written down, it may survive to be produced centuries later by a new group of interpreters.

The work of the dramatist is developed by the other artists who contribute to create a performance, most especially the actors. The players interpret the roles the author has created and make them come alive before an audience in

the theatre. Acting in the theatre is the most difficult and impermanent of the arts; and an actor's ability is witnessed only by those there to experience it. As Shakespeare wrote:

These our actors,
As I foretold you, were all spirits and
Are melted into air, into thin air ...
We are such stuff
As dreams are made on, and our little life
Is rounded with a sleep.

A theatrical performance today can take many different forms. It may be a very expensive production, with famous actors and actresses and the latest in sound and lighting techniques. Or it may be a simple performance by a small drama group in a draughty local hall. Whatever form a performance takes, it always provides entertainment. In this book, we shall look at twenty men and women whose skill in the art of theatre has brought pleasure to millions.

1

Aeschylus

In classical Greece, drama was part of an annual competitive festival between three of the country's leading poets. Each poet wrote a play in the traditional form, with one leading actor and a chorus, which explained and commented on the plot for the audience. He also composed his own music, devised his own dances and showed how he wanted the play performed. The best play was given an award called the *Victory*. The greatest and most successful of the classical dramatists was Aeschylus. He is known as the 'father of European drama' and he is believed to have written ninety plays. He won his first *Victory* in 484 BC and won twelve more before his death in 456 BC. He also, unusually, won prizes after his death when his plays were revived.

Aeschylus was born of noble parents at Eleusis (now Elevsís) west of Athens in about 525 BC. As a young man, he fought at the famous Battle of

525 BC	born at Eleusis (now Elevsís) west of Athens
490 BC	fought at the Battle of Marathon; *Suppliants* first performed
484 BC	won first *Victory*
472 BC	*The Persians*
469 BC	*Seven Against Thebes*
460 BC	*Prometheus Bound*
458 BC	*The Oresteia* trilogy
456 BC	dies in Sicily

Right *Clytemnestra, wife of Agamemnon, awaits her husband's return from the Trojan wars in* The Oresteia.

Marathon, where the Greek army scored a surprising and great victory over the mighty Persians. It is also thought that he was present at the sea battle which took place off Salamis in 480 BC. A detailed and convincing description of this naval action in his play *The Persians* suggests that he was there.

Although the plays of Aeschylus reflect the issues of his own day, the dramatist also drew on the famous Greek legends, the epic poems of Homer, and traditional verses. Aeschylus's great masterpiece is *The Oresteia*. This group of three plays tells of the murder of King Agamemnon by his wife and her lover at the end of the Trojan War, the revenge of their son Orestes, and his flight from the avenging Furies.

Aeschylus introduced important developments into classical theatre. He reduced the size of the chorus and brought in a second main actor, allowing far more dialogue in his plays. Aeschylus died in 456 BC, the greatest dramatist of his time.

Above *A classical theatre on the slope of the Acropolis in Athens.*

2

William Shakespeare

1559-1603	reign of Queen Elizabeth I
1564	born at Stratford-upon-Avon
1592	acquires growing reputation on London stage as actor and playwright
1594	first English history plays and Roman plays written
1598-1612	performed with the Lord Chamberlain's Men and later the King's Men at the Globe Theatre, Bankside; *Hamlet*, *Othello*, *King Lear*, *Macbeth* and other great plays written
1612	retires to Stratford-upon-Avon
1616	dies

William Shakespeare was the most outstanding writer in an age of great writers. Born in Stratford-upon-Avon in Warwickshire and an actor by profession, Shakespeare wrote thirty-six plays and many poems and sonnets. These plays have been translated into all the major languages of the world, and have been performed world-wide.

Shakespeare's mastery of language and skill as a playwright were supreme. His five-act plays were written very quickly, usually in verse, and seemingly with little correction. Many of the plays were produced to suit the requirements of his acting companies or for special occasions before the court of Queen Elizabeth 1. But it was the content of Shakespeare's plays that made them unique. His Roman dramas, like *Julius Caesar*, *Antony and Cleopatra*, and *Coriolanus*, and his cycle of plays about late medieval English kingship (*King John* to *Richard III*), presented great sweeps of history and examined the invigorating effects of power politics.

Right *The Globe Theatre, where many of Shakespeare's plays were first performed.*

These plays also told how destructive that power could be if badly managed or abused. Likewise, his late great tragedies, such as *Macbeth*, *Othello*, *King Lear* and *Hamlet*, tackled powerful psychological issues. These dramas show how particular individuals sought to overcome powerful forces both from within themselves and from outside. Macbeth, for instance, is desperate to be king, yet struggles with the knowledge that to achieve his aim he must murder the reigning king and bring in an age of tyranny. Hamlet is a young, enlightened, Renaissance prince who wants to avenge his father's death, but finds it difficult to resort to murder and detests the corruption of the court.

Shakespeare wrote many types of play, including comedies, histories and tragedies. But he is known as the world's most universal writer because the content of his plays – the examination of political issues or the joy and sorrow of human life – makes them as relevant and enjoyable today, in all societies, as they were four hundred years ago in Elizabethan England.

Above *King Lear (Anthony Hopkins) seizes his Fool (Roshan Seth) in the famous storm scene.*

Below *Bottom the weaver is magically transformed: a scene from* A Midsummer Night's Dream.

3

Molière

In seventeenth-century France, society revolved around the whims and demands of the most powerful and successful monarch of the age, King Louis XIV, the Sun King. Among the many entertainers at his court was the actor and writer Jean Baptiste Poquelin, who called himself Molière. He was chosen to produce dramas and to create masques and pageants in the halls and gardens of great palaces like Versailles. Molière's plays have stood the test of time and have become classics.

As a young man, Molière ran away from home and joined a theatrical company. For thirteen years, he toured the French provinces learning the craft of the actor, observing how people behaved, and writing plays which poked fun at the society of his day. In time, these lessons were put to good effect when he began to create his own gallery of classic comic characters, in plays such as *Tartuffe*, a study in pious hypocrisy, *Le Misanthrope* (The Miser), *Le*

Below *A scene from Molière's popular play* The School for Wives. *His plays were often performed for Louis XIV in the sumptuous palace of Versailles (far right).*

Bourgeois Gentilhomme (The Bourgeois Gentleman), and his last great success *Le Malade Imaginaire* (The Imaginary Illness). This play was written in 1673 to entertain the King and was a bright, mocking satire on the medical profession. Molière himself played the main role, Monsieur Argan, a character who thought he had every type of illness and was only happy when surrounded by quack doctors.

Molière was greatly admired for his skills as a writer and entertainer, but was often hated by those he ridiculed. He was saved from banishment from court because the King enjoyed his plays. In 1673, Molière was taken ill on stage while playing Argan in *Le Malade Imaginaire* and died that same night. As a non-practising Catholic and as an actor, he was refused a Christian burial. However, the King intervened. Although Church leaders would not allow a proper funeral ceremony, on a dark winter's evening, Molière's coffin was pulled through streets lined with silent spectators and buried in holy ground.

Above Le Misanthrope *is one of Molière's most famous plays.*

1622	born in Paris
1643	joins the Béjarts family of actors and forms the Illustre-Théâtre Company
1658	Molière's company entertains Louis XIV in the Louvre on 24 October
1665-7	*Tartuffe, Le Misanthrope, Georges Dandin* produced
1671	*Le Bourgeois Gentilhomme*
1672	*Le Malade Imaginaire*
1673	dies 17 February

4

Edmund Kean

The English actor Edmund Kean was one of the most exciting stage performers and the first to acquire a legendary international reputation. In the age of Romanticism, Kean impressed his audiences with the emotional power of his performances. 'To see Edmund Kean act', wrote the poet Samuel Taylor Coleridge, 'was like reading Shakespeare by flashes of lightning'. Lord Byron returned from seeing Kean in 1814 and noted in his journal 'Just returned from seeing Kean in *Richard III*. By Jove he is a soul! Life, nature, truth, without exaggeration or diminution'.

Kean was a classic example of the gifted actor, who, through unruly behaviour, conceit and alcoholism, destroyed both his career and himself.

He was born in London, the illegitimate son of an actress. Although his early childhood was desperately hard, he was able to acquire a thorough grounding in singing, dancing, fencing and

1787	born in London; becomes child actor, spends some years touring the provinces
1814 -26	January, makes London debut as Shylock in *The Merchant of Venice* at Drury Lane Theatre; years of success and international tours, followed by decline
1833	last role Othello at Covent Garden with his son, the actor Charles Kean, as Iago; dies15 May

acrobatics, the skills needed for a career in the theatre. His early years were spent touring in the provinces, but when he finally made his London debut, as Shylock in Shakespeare's *The Merchant of Venice*, at Drury Lane Theatre on 26 January 1814, the effect on the audience was electric. The great drama critic William Hazlitt recorded the event: 'The boxes were empty and the pit was half full. The whole theatre presented a dreary, hopeless, aspect. I was in considerable apprehension for the result. From the first scene in which Mr Kean came on my doubts were at an end. For voice, eye, action, and expression, no actor has come out for many years at all to equal him.'

Kean was at his most effective when he played characters who were strangely and wickedly fascinating, such as Shylock, Richard III, Othello, Macbeth, Iago, or Barabas in Marlowe's *The Jew of Malta*. In Kean's day audiences went to the theatre to be thrilled by star performers and few actors have ever matched Edmund Kean at his best.

Above *'Angels and ministers of grace defend us': Kean, as Hamlet, confronts the ghost of his father.*

Below *Kean plays the foolish king, Richard II, doomed to lose his throne and be murdered gruesomely.*

5

Henrik Ibsen

The plays of the Norwegian dramatist Henrik Ibsen were to have a profound effect on the history of western drama. His great works were close examinations of Norwegian society which probed into unpleasant and rarely discussed truths. Although many of his works were widely praised, he was strongly condemned for some of his more controversial plays and he was forced to live in exile for many years.

Ibsen's early efforts were verse plays, such as *Brand* and *Peer Gynt*, often containing a strong-willed, uncompromising hero; but it was a group of realistic prose dramas that were to have the greatest effect. These works examined the constraints and morals which existed in Norwegian and European society, and the feelings and behaviour often kept hidden from the outside world. His themes included the role of the downtrodden wife in *A Doll's House*, loose living and inherited venereal disease in *Ghosts*, and the

1828	born in Skien in south- east Norway
1851-7	joins National Theatre at Bergen and writes first verse dramas
1864-91	lives abroad, mainly in Italy and Germany
1866	*Brand* published, his first major success
1867	*Peer Gynt*
1877	*Pillars of Society*
1879-92	writes series of naturalistic prose plays including *A Doll's House*, *Ghosts*, *The Master Builder*
1906	dies in Christiania (now Oslo)

power of the individual will in *Hedda Gabler*. Some people welcomed this bold new approach to drama, but many others were shocked and Ibsen was attacked by the critics. One described *Ghosts* as 'one of the filthiest things ever written in Scandinavia'.

When Ibsen returned to Norway in 1891, he began a final series of plays which included *The Master Builder, Little Eyolf* and *When We Dead Awaken*. These powerful – and often disturbing – plays dealt with deep-rooted emotional and psychological problems.

Ibsen's lasting effect on drama was part of a wider movement towards realism among European playwrights of the era. The two other leading figures were his contemporaries August Strindberg and Anton Chekhov. The works of Strindberg, a Swede, are passionate and complicated. In contrast Chekhov, a Russian, was quiet and gentle but, nevertheless, truthful. Together with Ibsen, they moved drama firmly into the twentieth century.

Above *Hedvig and Gina comfort each other in a gloomy scene from* The Wild Duck.

Below *Peer Gynt takes his mother on an imaginary journey: a scene from one of Ibsen's early poetic dramas.*

6

Sarah Bernhardt

The nineteenth century was particularly notable for outstanding leading ladies. Internationally, the French actress Sarah Bernhardt became the most famous. She was a daring, tireless player, whose long tours throughout Europe, North and South America and Australia established her name world-wide.

Bernhardt was stunningly attractive. She had dark eyes, a shapely, slim figure, feline grace and a voice likened, by those who heard it, to 'the silver sound of running water' or to the sound of a 'golden bell'. Watching her rehearse his play *Le Sphinx*, the writer Octave Feuillet described Bernhardt as 'the real actress of the novels, the courtesan-actress of the eighteenth century, elegant, painted, eccentric and an insolent tomboy'.

Below *Performances in plays like* La Dame aux Camélias *made Bernhardt famous throughout the world.*

Although she was successful in *Phèdre*, by the French playwright Racine, and in Shakespeare's

Hamlet, her major successes came in less demanding roles, such as the dying courtesan Marguerite Gautier in Alexander Dumas's *La Dame aux Camélias*. She appeared most often in melodramas: some were even written specially for her. Audiences were enchanted by her dazzling performances and there were many scandalous and glamorous stories surrounding her private life. In some ways she was the nineteenth century's version of the Hollywood film star.

Paris was the artistic capital of the western world during Bernhardt's lifetime and she took advantage of it. A friend of artists, she was herself a talented poet, painter and sculptor. She also managed several of her own theatres and staged her own plays. She was, however, above all, a performer. 'I will die on stage,' she said, 'it is my battlefield.' Although one of her legs was amputated in 1915, she continued to perform on stage right up to her death in 1922.

Above *Bernhardt often played men's roles : one of her most famous was Hamlet.*

1844	born in Paris
1862	debut at the Théâtre Comédie Français
1872	first major success in Victor Hugo's *Ruy Blas*
1879	on tour in London with Racine's *Phèdre*
1880	in New York with *La Dame aux Camélias*
1898	produces own play *L'Aveu*
1909	produces own play *Un Coeur d'Homme*
1911	appears in film of *La Dame aux Camélias*
1915	leg amputated, continues playing in *Hamlet*
1922	dies in Paris

7

George Bernard Shaw

George Bernard Shaw was one of the most productive writers who has ever lived and one of the most active of men. He made public speeches, he was a journalist, a member of the socialist Fabian Society and he wrote many plays. When he died in 1950, aged ninety-four, he had written hundreds of political pamphlets and pieces of criticism, several books, thousands of letters, and over fifty dramatic works for the theatre, twenty of which are full-length masterpieces. These include *Arms and the Man*, *Man and Superman*, *Major Barbara*, *Pygmalion* and *Saint Joan*.

After an unhappy childhood, Shaw moved from his native Dublin to London in 1876 and began to develop the skill and enthusiasm for writing that were to make him a major literary figure. Shaw claimed to have no particular love for the theatre, but he could see its value as a way of expressing

Below *Shaw rehearses the leading actors in his play* Androcles and the Lion.

social and political ideas publicly. His plays use words very cleverly and his dialogues are witty and intelligent. Many of his early works reveal Shaw's views on issues of the day, such as prostitution in *Mrs Warren's Profession*, militarism and the arms race in *Arms and the Man* and *Heartbreak House*, and pacifism in *Carrington VC*.

Shaw was a great supporter of new drama, especially the translated works of Ibsen. He believed that, by dealing with social and moral problems, Ibsen's plays were bringing a stimulating breath of reality into the coy atmosphere of late-Victorian drama. Shaw wrote a book which emphasised his admiration for Ibsen's work; and to help spread the work of new and innovative playwrights, he took an active part in the running of the Court Theatre. This later became the Royal Court theatre and it continues to support the work of new, and sometimes controversial, playwrights today.

Above *Internationally celebrated: Shaw was one of the twentieth century's greatest literary figures.*

1856	born 26 July in Dublin, Ireland
1876	moves to London; begins period of self-education and writing
1884	joins the Fabian Society
1885	begins writing first play, *Widowers' Houses*
1904-7	Court Theatre seasons
1925	wins Nobel Prize for Literature
1950	2 November, dies at his home in Hertfordshire

8

Anton Chekhov

Russia's great playwright Anton Chekhov died in 1904, yet his plays are as fresh today as when he first wrote them. Chekhov wanted to bring about one major innovation: to put people on stage as they really were, naturally and without artifice.

In a short working life, Chekhov accomplished more than most other dramatists. He was a qualified and practising doctor, yet he also found time to write. He produced well over a thousand short stories, many of which are among the finest ever written. He wrote many amusing and skilful one-act plays, and hundreds of detailed, thoughtful letters full of ideas and plans. But his greatest fame rests on his half-dozen full-length plays, four of which are masterpieces: *The Seagull*, *Uncle Vanya*, *The Three Sisters* and *The Cherry Orchard*.

Like many innovators, Chekhov's plays were not widely understood when they were first performed. Even Constantin Stanislavsky, the

Below *Lopakhin, a businessman, persuades Madame Renyevskaya to sell her beloved estate in* The Cherry Orchard.

great Russian actor and director, admitted that he had little feeling for Chekhov's early work and little faith that it would be successful. But Chekhov was firm in his resolve, although it was frustrating for him to see how his plays were being misunderstood and often wrongly directed.

Chekhov was determined to get away from the theatrical, melodramatic and exaggerated style of much traditional playwriting and performance. He wanted to do what Shakespeare had advised in *Hamlet* centuries before: 'To hold, as 'twere, a mirror up to nature'. Chekhov said: 'The whole thing is very simple. The characters are simple, ordinary people. All I wanted was to tell people honestly "Look at yourselves"'. In tightly constructed, beautifully-styled pieces of writing, Chekhov portrayed ordinary human beings in their own environment. He captured the joy and pain of living, and, in particular, the petty frustrations experienced by country people in Tsarist Russia at the turn of the nineteenth century.

Above *The first performance of* Uncle Vanya, *at the famous Moscow Arts Theatre, in 1899.*

1860	born in Taganrog, on the sea of Azov
1887	*Ivanov* produced
1896	first performance of *The Seagull*
1897	becomes ill with tuberculosis
1898	*The Seagull* produced at the Moscow Arts Theatre
1899	*Uncle Vanya* produced
1901	*The Three Sisters* produced
1904	*The Cherry Orchard* produced dies in German spa town of Badenweiler

9

Eugene O'Neill

Eugene O'Neill was America's first great dramatist. He was a playwright of genuine force and originality, whose work dominated the American theatre scene for four decades until after the Second World War.

O'Neill was born into a theatrical family: his father and brother were both actors. His father played the Count of Monte Cristo for twenty years but O'Neill had no respect for such melodramatic forms of drama. He wanted to write plays that were truthful, with dialogue that was accurate and true to life. Many of his plays had an important influence on American drama. Some of his finest works are those in which he drew on his experiences at sea. These include *Beyond the Horizon* and *The Hairy Ape*. In others, he re-creates the desperately painful experiences of his own family

life, as in *Long Day's Journey into Night*. O'Neill would lock himself in his study for days on end in order to write this powerful work, emerging with tears running down his cheeks, saying 'It's too much to bear; I can't go on'. He would not allow the play to be performed until after his death.

To O'Neill the theatre was deeply serious. Plays had to tackle what he described as 'the big issues'. These dramas had to be daring, imaginative works, that could be compared with the great tragedies of Greek theatre. His *Mourning Becomes Electra*, is, in fact, a retelling of the tragic tale of King Agamemnon, Clytemnestra, Orestes and Electra. In 1922, O'Neill wrote: 'The theatre to me is life, the substance and interpretation of life. And life is a struggle, often an unsuccessful struggle; for most of us have something within us which prevents us from accomplishing what we dream and desire. It is the dream that keeps us fighting, willing, living.'

1888	born in New York City
1916	first plays put on by the Provincetown Players at Provincetown, Massachusetts *Beyond the Horizon, The Emperor Jones* first performed
1922	*The Hairy Ape* produced
1924	*All God's Chillun Got Wings* and *Desire under the Elms*
1926	*The Great God Brown*
1931	*Mourning Becomes Electra*
1933	*Ah Wilderness*
1936	wins Nobel Prize for Literature
1939-41	*Long Day's Journey into Night* written (not produced until 1956)
1946	*The Iceman Cometh*
1947	*A Moon for the Misbegotten*
1953	dies in Boston

Left *Laurence Olivier in his last great stage role as James Tyrone, in O'Neill's* Long Day's Journey Into Night. *Denis Quilley played his drunkard son, Jamie.*

10

The Lunts

Men and women actors have often formed partnerships, appearing together in performance. Examples from the nineteenth century include Henry Irving and Ellen Terry and, from the twentieth century, Laurence Olivier and Vivien Leigh. None, however, was more dedicated and admired than the partnership of the English-born actress Lynne Fontanne and her American husband, Alfred Lunt, known as the Lunts.

The Lunts began their careers independently and were successful in their own countries. Even after their marriage in 1922, they occasionally performed in separate productions: in 1926, Fontanne was a brilliant Eliza Doolittle in Shaw's *Pygmalion* and Lunt a success in a play called *Ned McCobb's Daughter*. There is no doubt, however, that they were at their best when they acted with each other.

The Lunts began their partnership when they were involved with the Theatre Guild of New York

in the 1920s. In 1924, they were a great success in a play by a Hungarian dramatist, Ferenc Molnár, called *The Guardsman*. They performed together again in Shaw's *Arms and the Man* in 1925 and in 1926 appeared in *The Brothers Karamazov*, a stage-version of the novel by the Russian writer, Dostoevsky. After leaving the Theatre Guild in 1929, they began to promote their own productions. They had many great successes including, for instance, *Design For Living*, by the English actor and dramatist Noël Coward, who wrote several popular plays between the two World Wars. Their last big triumph was with *The Visit*, by the Swiss playwright Friedrich Dürrenmatt: it opened in New York in 1958 and in London in 1960.

The Lunts' success can be put down to two basic principles: total dedication to the art of acting, which involves conserving energy for the daily performance; and practising the craft constantly in order to make every performance as natural and truthful as possible.

Above *The Lunts share centre-stage in the Broadway production of* Caprice.

1887	Lynne Fontanne born
1892	Alfred Lunt born
1905	Fontanne makes stage debut works with Ellen Terry and Sir Herbert Beerhbolm Tree in London
1910	Fontanne travels to New York
1913	Alfred Lunt makes stage debut
1922	Fontanne and Lunt marry
1924-9	Theatre Guild productions
1929-60	they act together in successful productions
1977	Alfred Lunt dies
1983	Lynne Fontanne dies

11

Paul Robeson

Paul Robeson, the American singer, actor, and civil rights campaigner, was the first black performer to achieve great international fame. His rich, deep bass voice is well known from his recordings of the song 'Ol' Man River', from Jerome Kern's musical, *Show Boat*, in which he starred in 1928. His fine acting ability was revealed when he appeared in three plays by Eugene O'Neill, *All God's Chillun Got Wings*, *The Emperor Jones* and *The Hairy Ape*; and when he first appeared as Shakespeare's *Othello* in London in 1930.

Robeson was born in Princeton, New Jersey, where his father, once a runaway slave, was a Presbyterian minister. He went to Columbia University to study law but his acting and singing abilities took him into the world of entertainment. He made his acting debut in 1920, while still a student, in a play called *Simon the Cyrenean*. In New

Below *Robeson in his most famous role, Othello, with Peggy Ashcroft as Desdemona.*

York, he began singing at the Cotton Club in Harlem. He made recordings and continued to give performances of negro songs for the rest of his life, often on tour.

Robeson was deeply political and felt strongly about the plight of black people in the USA. He spoke out against racial discrimination and segregation, and did not hide the fact that he was a communist. During the 1950s, many Americans suspected of being communists were persecuted by the House UnAmerican Activities Committee (HUAC), led by Senator Joseph McCarthy. Robeson himself had his passport taken away and American producers were reluctant to employ him. However, he was not forgotten. In 1949, the Soviet Union named a mountain after him and, in 1952, awarded him the Stalin Peace Prize. Robeson played *Othello* for the last time at Stratford-upon-Avon in 1959, when he was sixty-one, and his performance was very well received.

Above *Robeson in the title role of Eugene O'Neill's powerful play* The Emperor Jones.

1898	born Princeton, New Jersey, USA
1920	makes stage debut in *Simon the Cyrenean*
1924	stars in *All God's Chillun Got Wings*
1925	Cotton Club gramophone recordings made; plays lead in *The Emperor Jones*
1928	*Show Boat* produced
1930	plays *Othello* in London
1931	stars in *The Hairy Ape*
1934	first visit to Moscow
1949	plays *Othello* in USA
1950-58	passport revoked by US Government
1956	appears before HUAC
1976	dies

12

Bertolt Brecht

The German Marxist playwright, Bertolt Brecht, was not only an innovative theatre director, but was also the most influential political dramatist of the twentieth century. He detested the elaborate productions of German theatre and was fiercely and courageously opposed to Adolf Hitler and Nazism. Brecht's plays are filled with his political ideas, like his anti-war drama, *Trumpets and Drums*, and his group of anti-Hitler plays, including *The Resistible Rise of Arturo Ui*. His later works are his finest. *Galileo* tells of the defeat of the great scientist by the Church. In *Mother Courage and Her Children*, Mother Courage tries to protect her family during the Thirty Years' War but fails in the end when the war destroys her children. In *The Caucasian Chalk Circle*, simple good-heartedness defeats the political system.

To promote his ideas, Brecht devised a new way to stage his plays which did away with elaborate

Below *Scenes from Brecht's play* The Good Woman of Setzuan.

scenery. The staging was simple and a backcloth was used to reflect a single, relevant dominating image, such as the twin-towers of *The Caucasian Chalk Circle* or Mother Courage's covered wagon. Each scene in a Brecht play was prefaced by a projected caption which presented the audience with information or opinion. Brecht called his new technique 'Epic Theatre'.

Brecht also devised an original way of performing his plays which was intended to prevent actors from identifying too closely with their roles. Brecht encouraged his actors to consider themselves to be just like any other workers. The actor's job was to tell stories, in the same way as there were workers whose job it was to dig ditches: no more, no less. Brecht did not want to create a theatre of illusion and mystery. He wanted to make his audience aware of where they were and what they were seeing. The result was that Brecht's company, the Berliner Ensemble, reached performance skills rarely seen before or since.

Above *Brecht at work with the composer, Paul Dessau.*

1899	born Augsburg, Bavaria
1918	writes first play *Baal*
1928	first night of *The Threepenny Opera*
1930	first night of *The Rise and Fall of the City of Mahagonny*
1933	Adolf Hitler assumes power in Germany; Brecht lives abroad
1948	returns to Europe upon founding of socialist state of East Germany
1949	founds the Berliner Ensemble in East Berlin
1956	14 August, dies

13

Peggy Ashcroft

1907	born in Croydon, England
1929	first stage success in *Jew Süss*
1930	plays Desdemona to Paul Robeson's Othello in London
1935	plays Juliet to Olivier's and Gielgud's Romeo
1940s	plays many classical roles
1956	created Dame of the British Empire
1960	joins Royal Shakespeare Company
1985	wins BAFTA award for best actress role in *The Jewel in the Crown* and *A Passage To India*

The great English actress Dame Edith Evans once described how she created a role: 'I speak the truth. When I was a young girl I was taught to speak the truth at all times and that is what I do with a part. I study the character and find out what she has to say, and then I speak the lines as truthfully as I possibly can.' These words would equally sum up the approach of Peggy Ashcroft. She works steadily until she finds the truth of every role inside herself, simplifying until only the bare essentials remain.

Peggy Ashcroft was born in Surrey and trained for the stage at the Central School of Drama in London, where Laurence Olivier was a fellow student. Her first big success was as Naemi in the romantic drama *Jew Süss* in 1929. She has remained at the forefront of British acting ever since and has played most of the great Shakespearian women's roles. She was an outstanding success as

Right *Ashcroft (inset) as Queen Margaret in* The Wars of the Roses *and as Beatrice in Shakespeare's* Much Ado About Nothing.

Desdemona in *Othello* and as Juliet in *Romeo and Juliet*. She has played the great roles of Ibsen, including the title role in *Hedda Gabler*, and has portrayed many of the famous female characters of Chekhov's plays, such as Madame Arkadina in *The Seagull*.

Although Peggy Ashcroft has had great success in productions in London's West End, she prefers to work with a company that has a clear identity and in 1960 she became a founder member of the Royal Shakespeare Company. She is more interested in ensemble playing than in appearing in plays which spotlight only the star actors.

In 1956, Peggy Ashcroft was made a Dame of the British Empire in recognition of her services to the theatre. More recently, her acting skills have reached a wider audience due to many successful television and film appearances, including her award-winning roles in *A Passage To India* and *The Jewel in the Crown*.

Above *A pensive moment for Ashcroft in a scene from Chekhov's* The Three Sisters.

14

Laurence Olivier

Laurence Olivier is considered the twentieth century's greatest man of the theatre. In a glittering career lasting over sixty years, he has been a splendid bravura actor, a Hollywood star, a stage director, an actor-manager, the first director of Britain's National Theatre, and the man whose films brought Shakespeare to a world-wide audience.

The son of a clergyman, Olivier showed his acting ability at an early age. The once-famous actress, Ellen Terry, who saw the ten-year-old Olivier play Brutus in a school production of *Julius Caesar*, wrote in her diary, 'The small boy who played Brutus is already a great actor!'

Olivier has always been a great impersonator. In every role he played he wanted to show his versatility, and to make the audience believe that he was a different person every time. For instance, when he played one of his most famous roles, Shakespeare's Richard III, he based his make-up on

1907	born Dorking, England
1935	appears in *Romeo and Juliet*
1932-40	features in many films in Britain and USA
1944	appointed joint artistic director of the Old Vic Company
1944-50	great theatrical seasons with Ralph Richardson; directs the films of *Henry V*, *Hamlet* and *Richard III*
1963	appointed first director of Britain's National Theatre
1972	retires as National Theatre director
1973-88	appears in films including *Sleuth*, *The Boys from Brazil* and others and in major TV productions

the wolf-like features of a very unpleasant director whom he disliked and his voice on that of the actor Sir Henry Irving.

Olivier had all the gifts and skills to play the big demanding roles. As a young man he was strikingly handsome, with a magnetic stage presence. He could control an audience and had the ability to communicate a sense of danger. No other actor of this century has succeeded in playing the range of parts that he has. They include Oedipus in *Oedipus Rex* by Sophocles, and all the great Shakespearian roles, notably Hamlet, Henry V, Richard III, Othello, Macbeth and Coriolanus. He has also played the leading roles in John Osborne's *The Entertainer*, Chekhov's *Uncle Vanya*, O'Neill's *Long Day's Journey into Night* and many others.

Olivier's theatrical achievements (and, more recently, his television roles) have inspired generations of young actors. In 1947, he was knighted for his services to the theatre and, in 1970, he was created Baron Olivier of Brighton, the first actor ever to sit in the House of Lords.

Above *In his dressing room, Olivier prepares for his role as Oedipus in Sophocles' tragedy,* Oedipus Rex.

Below (left) *Olivier as Richard III, one of his most famous roles, and, (right) as Archie Rice, performing his song and dance routine in* The Entertainer.

15

Arthur Miller

In the years immediately after the Second World War, the USA produced an outstanding playwright whose major works have become classics of modern drama. Arthur Miller began writing plays at university and won several prizes. In 1944, one of his plays, *The Man Who Had All The Luck*, was produced on Broadway, but it flopped and was taken off after only a week; for a while it seemed that Miller's luck had run out.

However, success on Broadway came three years later with *All My Sons*. It was followed by *Death of a Salesman*, *The Crucible* and A *View from the Bridge*. Most of Miller's work springs from personal experiences or reflects his response to real events. Willie Loman, the small man with a great dream in *Death of a Salesman*, for instance, was based on a man who worked for Miller's father.

Below *New York longshoreman, Eddie Carbone, taunts the young immigrant, Rodolpho, in* A View from the Bridge.

Miller has always been particularly outspoken in his opposition to political persecution. When the notorious Senator Joseph McCarthy and the House UnAmerican Activities Committee (HUAC) began to accuse Miller and his friends of being communists and betraying their country, Miller responded by writing his great historical drama, *The Crucible*. This play dramatized the horrific witch-hunt trials which occurred in Salem, Massachusetts, in 1692. Respected people in this small Christian community were falsely accused of witchcraft and (like many of Miller's friends, over two hundred years later,) were convicted without evidence. The victims in *The Crucible* were executed for crimes they did not commit. Yet, because Miller wrote about their courage and defiance, his play helped to counter the fear, distrust, and persecution in his own society. Indeed, in many of his plays, Miller is the social conscience of his time.

Above *Miller attends the British premiere of* A View from the Bridge, *with his wife Marilyn Monroe.*

1915	born New York City
1944	*The Man Who Had All The Luck* performed on Broadway
1947	*All My Sons* performed
1949	*Death of a Salesman*
1950-54	McCarthy trials
1953	*The Crucible*
1955	A *View from the Bridge*
1956	marries Marilyn Monroe, his second wife (divorced 1961)
1957	convicted of contempt for refusing to give names of known communists to HUAC hearings.
1964	*After the Fall* *Incident at Vichy*
1968	*The Price*
1977	*The Archbishop's Ceiling*
1980	*The American Clock*

16

Christopher Plummer

Below right *Plummer, as Richard of Gloucester, woos Lady Anne in the RSC'S 1961 production of* Richard III.

1929	born Toronto
1954	New York debut
1950s-60s	plays leading roles at Stratford, Ontario; Stratford, Connecticut; and with Royal Shakespeare Company in England
1961	Award for best actor as Henry II in Anouillh's *Becket*
1971	season with the National Theatre of Great Britain
1981	plays Iago with the American Shakespeare Theatre
1988	plays Macbeth on Broadway

Christopher Plummer is a Canadian actor who has made an outstanding contribution to the international stage. Since making his theatrical debut in 1950, he has played a wide range of roles and is now one of the leading actors of his generation.

The great stage director Tyrone Guthrie, who directed Plummer in many performances, wrote that only by playing the classic roles could the skill of a performer be measured. By this he meant that these roles make such demands upon performers that their imagination and physical capabilities are tested to the full. Like Olivier before him, Christopher Plummer has many advantages which help him to excel in the great roles. He is athletic and handsome. He has a powerful voice that can express a great range of feelings, and an impressive stage presence.

Plummer has demonstrated his versatility as an actor by playing the leading roles in a wide range

of Shakespeare's plays, including the great tragedies and the Roman plays such as *Julius Caesar* and *Antony and Cleopatra*. He is equally at home in comedies, playing such characters as Benedick in *Much Ado about Nothing*. One of his finest – and most exhausting – performances was in *Henry V*, when he played both the title role and the part of the Chorus. He has also appeared in several plays by twentieth-century writers. These include performances as Henry II in *Becket*, by the French dramatist Jean Anouillh; as the Spanish adventurer Pizzarro in Peter Shaffer's play *The Royal Hunt of the Sun* and the title role in Brecht's *The Resistible Rise of Arturo Ui*.

Although he continues to work in the theatre, having recently appeared in a Broadway production of *Macbeth*, Plummer has also starred in a number of films. These include *The Royal Hunt of the Sun*, *Night of the Generals* and the enormously popular *The Sound of Music*. His performance as Captain von Trapp in this film made him internationally famous.

Above *Christopher Plummer, seen here in a dramatic moment from the film* The Disappearance *(1981).*

17

Harold Pinter

Harold Pinter's early plays were often called 'comedies of menace'. *The Room*, *The Birthday Party*, *The Dumb Waiter*, *The Caretaker*, and *The Homecoming* were placed in working-class settings, either in dingy bed-sitting rooms or houses in run-down neighbourhoods. Against these backgrounds, the characters in the plays are subjected to extreme terror, violence or humiliation. Pinter's later plays expand to include a sexual element as in *The Lover*, or the changing states of memory, as in *Betrayal* and *A Kind of Alaska*.

Harold Pinter was born in Hackney in the East End of London of Jewish parents. He remembers clearly as a schoolboy the fear, the threats, and the violence of life in London's East End in the 1930s. Sir Oswald Mosley's black-shirted Fascists fought with those who supported communism. These events had a profound effect upon Pinter. In the years following the Second World War, after a brief spell of training to be an actor, Pinter toured in

Below *Brothers Aston and Mick, tease the tramp, Davies, in a scene from* The Caretaker, *one of Pinter's most famous plays.*

Ireland, and later appeared in Shakespeare's plays in London. It was in the late 1950s that he first had success as a playwright.

The vague, shadowy world of Pinter's best work is clearly influenced by the unexplained settings of the Irish playwright Samuel Beckett, in such works as *Waiting for Godot*, and by the strange, overpowering scenes created by Franz Kafka, in such novels as *The Castle*. Much of Pinter's dialogue is influenced by the poetry of T.S. Eliot, a twentieth-century writer whom Pinter greatly admired.

Pinter's writing is straightforward and he is always concerned with finding the right structure for his plays. This helps to produce concentrated and controlled performances from the actors. Pinter's ability to edit and produce good dialogue has also made him into a fine adaptor of other people's novels for the cinema. His most successful screenplays include adaptations of *The Servant*, *The Pumpkin Eater*, *The Go-Between*, and *The French Lieutenant's Woman*.

Above *As well as being a prolific playwright, Pinter has written screenplays for some of the best films of the last twenty years.*

1930	born 10 October in Hackney, London
1957	*The Room* produced
1958	*The Birthday Party*
1960	*The Dumb Waiter* *The Caretaker*
1961-3	one-act plays *A Slight Ache*, *The Collection*, *The Lover*
1965	*The Homecoming*
1968-9	*Landscape* and *Silence*
1971	*Old Times*
1975	*No Man's Land*
1978	*Betrayal*
1982	triple bill of one-act plays, including *A Kind of Alaska*
1988	*Mountain Language*

18

Maggie Smith

Few actresses in the world today are as adept at playing both high comedy and serious drama as Maggie Smith. A twitch from her slim figure, a puzzled look, or the delivery of a line spoken in her distinctive nasal voice, can make an audience explode into uproarious laughter. She controls her audiences expertly by knowing the exact moment to deliver the comic riposte.

Maggie Smith began performing in revue and then went on to play more serious roles with the Old Vic Company. In 1960, she played opposite Laurence Olivier in *Rhinoceros* by Eugene Ionesco. Later, she received awards for her roles in *The Private Ear* and *The Public Eye* by Peter Shaffer. In these plays, she worked with the splendid comic actor, Kenneth Williams, whose characteristically exaggerated way of speaking was somewhat similar to her own.

Below *Maggie Smith as Hedda Gabler in the National Theatre's 1970 production of Ibsen's drama.*

Her career took a big leap forward when she was invited to join the newly-established National Theatre Company in 1963. Here she played many of the major female roles and gave some splendid performances. She was, for instance, wonderfully sophisticated and humorous, yet determined, as Ibsen's Hedda Gabler.

For the last twenty years, Maggie Smith has combined a stage career with leading parts in films, including her Oscar-winning performance as Jean Brodie in *The Prime of Miss Jean Brodie* and, more recently, her role as Charlotte Bartlett in *A Room With A View*. At Stratford, Ontario, she played the sparklingly comic role of Beatrice in Shakespeare's *Much Ado About Nothing* and Madame Arkadina in *The Seagull*, by Chekhov. Her outstanding talent was on show again when she appeared in Shaffer's *Lettice and Lovage*. Maggie Smith is one of only a small number of British actresses who have enjoyed great success on stage and in film.

Above *Maggie Smith and Richard Pearson in the London production of Peter Shaffer's* Lettice and Lovage.

1934	born in Essex, England
1959	Old Vic seasons
1962	*The Private Ear* and *The Public Eye*
1963	joins National Theatre Company
1968	award-winning performance in film *The Prime of Miss Jean Brodie*
1970s	appears in productions at Stratford Festival Theatre, Ontario
1984	*The Way of the World* at Chichester Festival Theatre
1986/7	*Coming in to Land*
1987/8	*Lettice and Lovage* in London

19

Vanessa Redgrave

In the world of the theatre, there have been a number of notable families who have, for generations, contributed to the history of the stage. Among the most famous are the Redgraves. Sir Michael Redgrave was one of England's most notable actors, and was himself the son and grandson of touring performers. He married an actress, Rachel Kempson, and they, in turn, produced three children, all of whom became actors. The most talented of the three is their eldest child, Vanessa, born in 1937.

Vanessa Redgrave is an outstanding actress of unusual individuality and truthfulness. She is noticeably tall and commanding with a splendid radiance. She first came to public notice in 1961 when she played a sparkling and moving Rosalind in Shakespeare's *As You Like It* at Stratford-upon-Avon. Later, she appeared in productions of Ibsen's plays, being particularly praised for her performance as Ellida in *The Lady from the Sea*.

Below *Vanessa Redgrave and Timothy Dalton as Nora and Cornelius Melody in Eugene O'Neill's drama* A Touch of the Poet.

Another of her early successes was the role of the schoolmistress, Miss Jean Brodie, in the stage-version of Muriel Spark's novel *The Prime of Miss Jean Brodie*. Redgrave was charming, witty and tragic in her playing of this very romantic and idealistic, but misguided, heroine.

Vanessa Redgrave is also well known for her commitment to the left-wing Worker's Revolutionary Party and to the Palestinian cause, and for her roles in films, such as *Agatha*, *The Bostonians*, *Wetherby* and *Camelot*. Many of these activities have prevented her from fulfilling her early theatrical promise, although in the 1980s she has occasionally returned to the stage. In recent years she has portrayed characters as varied and interesting as Madame Arkadina in Chekhov's *The Seagull*, Cleopatra in Shakespeare's *Antony and Cleopatra*, Mrs. Alving in Ibsen's *Ghosts* and the downtrodden wife in Eugene O'Neill's *A Touch of the Poet*. The Redgrave theatrical tradition continues with Vanessa's own two daughters who have also become actresses.

Above *Redgrave as Madame Arkadina, with her daughter, Natasha Richardson, as Nina in Chekhov's* The Seagull.

1937	born in Blackheath, London, 30 January
1957	makes stage debut
1961	plays Rosalind in *As You Like It*
1966	title role in the West End production of *The Prime of Miss Jean Brodie*
1970s	film roles
1980s	leading stage roles in *The Aspern Papers*, *The Seagull*, *Antony and Cleopatra*, *The Taming of the Shrew*, *Ghosts*, and *A Touch of the Poet.*
1988-9	appears in *Orpheus Descending*

20

Al Pacino

The Broadway stage has produced many fine actors who have gone on to greater international success by making films in Hollywood. Some of those performers have returned to the stage. Others have managed to keep up their skills in both mediums. Of the younger generation of American actors, Al Pacino has most successfully combined the arts of stage and screen acting.

Pacino was born of a Sicilian family in Manhattan, New York and grew up in The Bronx. As a young man, he showed a talent for acting and attended the New York High School of Performing Arts. Later, he studied under Charles Laughton and trained at the Actors' Studio. He made his theatrical debut in Chekhov's *The Seagull*, and went on to perform with the Living Theatre Company. Later, he played the lead roles in Brecht's *Arturo Ui* and Shakespeare's Richard II with the Boston Theatre

Below *Al Pacino in the role of Teacher in David Mamet's powerful contemporary play,* American Buffalo.

Company. By the later 1960s, Pacino had begun to make his mark in New York and won several awards for his acting.

It was during this period that Pacino began to be offered a series of film roles that were to make him an international star. He made his debut in *Panic in Needle Park* but his finest film performance to date was as Michael Corleone in the two parts of *The Godfather*. In this role, Pacino demonstrated a quiet, almost sinister, power and strength, as he became head of the Corleone family following the death of his father, played by Marlon Brando.

His reputation established, Pacino returned to the stage, playing Shakespeare's Richard III and Mark Antony in *Julius Caesar*. His most notable performance was as Teacher in David Mamet's *American Buffalo*. In this contemporary play, set in a junk-shop, Pacino proved himself to be a stage actor with a powerful presence, a strong, resonant voice and great control over an audience.

Above *Al Pacino, seen here in the film* Scarecrow, *has successfully combined the arts of screen and stage acting.*

1940	born New York attends High School of Performing Arts; makes debut in *The Seagull*
1969	Tony Award for *Does A Tiger Wear A Necktie?*
1972	Tony Award for *The Basic Training of Pavlo Hummel*; appears in film *The Godfather*
1973	*Serpico, The Godfather Part II*
1984	appears in *American Buffalo* in New York and London
1988	appears in *Julius Caesar*

Glossary

Actors' Studio Training centre in New York.
Artifice Special tricks, skills or devices.
Backcloth A painted canvas which hangs at the back of a scene, suspended from the theatre grid in the roof of the theatre.
BAFTA British Academy of Film and Television Arts.
Bravura Brilliant, ambitious and bold acting.
Broadway Famous avenue in New York where most of the theatres are located.
Courtesan A prostitute in upper-class society.
Delivery The way an actor/actress says the lines.
Director The person who interprets what an author has written, and helps the actors to perform their parts in the best way possible.
Ensemble A company dedicated to playing together as a group, and avoiding 'star' performances.
Fascists Supporters of the extreme right wing policies of Hitler and Mussolini. Many British Fascists were members of the British Union, led by Sir Oswald Mosley.
House UnAmerican Activities Committee A United States national committee ordered to seek out communists in government service, and in prominent and influential positions in the entertainment industry. In operation from the later 1940s to 1950s.
Marxism Social, economic and political beliefs based on the theories of Karl Marx.
Masque An amateur court entertainment with music.
Melodrama A play, often a romance, with sensational incidents and extravagant emotion.
Nazism Tyrannical policies of the German National Socialist Party led by Adolf Hitler, in power from 1933 to 1945.
Producer The person who finances a stage production.
Realism Artistic movement which attempts to illustrate life as it really is.
Revue A light entertainment composed of short scenes, mainly satirizing contemporary events.
Riposte Quick, sharp reply.
Romanticism An artistic, literary and dramatic movement which developed in the early nineteenth century. In the theatre the imaginative and passionate performances of actors like Kean became popular.
Segregation Policy of enforcing white and black people to live apart.
Tony Annual award given for the best performance or contribution to a New York stage show.

Further reading

All the World's a Stage by Ronald Harwood (Secker & Warburg, 1984)
Backstage: who does what in the theatre by Judith Cook (Harrap, 1987)
Being an Actor by Simon Callow (Penguin, 1985)
Confessions of an Actor by Laurence Olivier (Weidenfeld & Nicolson, 1982)
On Acting by Laurence Olivier (Weidenfeld & Nicolson, 1987)
Shakespeare by Christopher Martin (Wayland, 1988)
Theatre by Howard Loxton (Wayland, 1989)
Twenty Names in Modern Literature by Edwina Conner (Wayland, 1987)
William Shakespeare by Christopher Martin (Wayland, 1988)

Index

Picture acknowledgements:

Aquarius 45; BBC Hulton Picture Library 15, 19, 27, 29, 31; Camera Press 41, 43; Mary Evans Picture Library 11, 13, 17; Jimmy Holmes 7; Kobal Collection 37; Mander & Mitchenson 25; Popperfoto 33; Topham Picture Library 35, 39; Wayland Picture Library 8, 9, 21.